What The Devil Saw On The Day Of Pentecost

Rev. Michael Fram

Acknowledgements

I am indebted to the Ministry leaders of the Body of Christ who have impacted me and spoken into my life and ministry through the years by precept and example.

Dr. Leo & Rev. Edith Fram – my Parents and two of the best mentors any son could ever ask for, because they live what they preach, make opportunities for those upcoming, and give correcting council along the way.

Rev. Kenneth E. (Dad) Hagin – impacted my life through sitting at his feet during my two years at Rhema Bible Training Center as well as through his books and tapes.

Rev. Billy Joe Daugherty – most likely the greatest example I have ever witnessed on this earth of a true Pastor with a real genuine Shepard's heart. One of the most humble men I have ever met.

Table of Contents

Preface

I have been a student of the Holy Spirit for many years. In fact there was a ten year period in my life that the Holy Spirit was all I studied. Every book I bought and read dealt with the subject matter of the Holy Spirit. Most of my times of mediation were spent pondering the ministry of the Holy Spirit.

I came to the place that I realized that everything Jesus did in His earthly ministry was because He was anointed by the Holy Spirit. Conversely everything that we will do will be the same way. If Jesus needed to be anointed by the Holy Spirit, how much more do we?

This book originally started as a sermon that I have been preaching for about 20 years. Over the years as my revelation grew into the truth of the word of God, the message grew in revelation as well.

Through the years the response to this message has always been extremely positive. In fact many times people have told me that I should turn it into a book. Over the last few years I have received many prophetic words about writing. One in particular said: "*Write Michael, write.*"

When God speaks the same thing to you over and over again it is wise to obey His instruction. A couple of years ago after preaching this message to a group of folks who never heard it before, my Mom came to me and said that should be your first book.

So I began to work on this book little by little. What you hold in your hands is the result of over twenty years of study and revelation. I pray these truths will change you as they have changed me.

Come with me on a journey to discover: "What The Devil Saw On The Day Of Pentecost."

Introduction

Pentecost is an important part of both the New Testament Church as well as the Old Testament history of the church's Jewish roots. Pentecost is one of three major feasts in the Jewish calendar, the other two being Passover and The Feast of Tabernacles. These three feasts and other festivals make up what is described in Leviticus 23 as appointed times.

"Speak to the sons of Israel and say to them, 'The LORD'S **appointed times** *which you shall proclaim as holy convocations--My* **appointed times** *are these..."* **Leviticus 23:2 NASB**

Pentecost is one of the appointed times listed. The Hebrew word for appointed time is transliterated, Moadim or Mow'ed, which means appointed place, appointed time, appointed meeting, sacred season, set feast, appointed season. God has set Pentecost as one of His appointed times to the children of Israel, and so it should come as no surprise to us that He would do something major on one of His own appointed times.

God did major things for the birth of the New Testament Church at Jewish appointed times. The crucifixion came at Passover time, which signified the end of the Old Covenant need for animal sacrifices, since the spotless Lamb of God had laid down His life. On Pentecost came the mighty outpouring of the Holy Spirit fulfilling Joel's prophecy and what Jesus had declared just before His ascension in Acts 1:8.

Pentecost simply means fifty. Pentecost came fifty days after Passover. We in the church look back at Acts chapter two to The Day of Pentecost as one of the pivotal events of church history. In this book we'll explore The Day of Pentecost from a different viewpoint.

Let's look at Pentecost from Satan's perspective. Suppose you or I were the devil (thank God we're not, but suppose we were) what does Pentecost look like? What do we see? How does it look to us?

I think if the church could get a glimpse of Pentecost from the devil's point of view we would realize what we have in a whole new light. We would have a greater appreciation for what God has provided for us in the Pentecostal experience.

Take a journey with me into a viewpoint you may have never considered before and see if God does not give you some great revelation that absolutely blesses you beyond words.

Chapter I
The Prelude To Pentecost

"When the day of Pentecost had come, they were all together in one place. And suddenly there came from heaven a noise like a violent rushing wind, and it filled the whole house where they were sitting. And there appeared to them tongues as of fire distributing themselves, and they rested on each one of them. And they were all filled with the Holy Spirit and began to speak with other tongues, as the Spirit was giving them utterance." **Acts 2:1-4 NASB**

Before we can really understand the impact of Pentecost for us in the church, and the impact it had on Satan's kingdom, we must understand what transpired between the Crucifixion and the Resurrection. Failure to understand what transpired between these two events will cause us to miss the importance and relevance of Pentecost altogether.

Death On Three Levels

When the Bible speaks of death, there are three types of death that are depicted. First there is physical death, which means the cessation of life. Second there is spiritual death, which means separation from God. Finally there is the "Second Death" or eternal judgment, which is damnation and punishment in hell.

Go with me in your mind to the Garden of Eden. God told Adam and Eve that they could eat of any tree in the garden except for the tree of the knowledge of good and evil in the center of the garden. Any of the other trees were fine just not that one. If you will that tree was a tithe that belonged to the Lord. (That is a whole nother teaching that we won't get into now)

God said that the day you eat of that tree you shall surely die. Isn't that what God said? Now the serpent came and said has God really said that? Yes God did really say that and He meant it! We know that Adam and Eve both ate of the fruit of the tree that God said not to eat from. Did they die?

If God said that if they ate from the tree they would surely die...how come Adam lived to be over 900 years old?

*"So all the **days** that **Adam** lived were **nine hundred and thirty years**, and he died."* **Genesis 5:5 NASB**

I thought God said the day that he ate he would surely die. Well we know that it is impossible for God to lie (Hebrews 6:18) so if Adam did not die physically, how did he die? What type of death did he experience? Since God cannot lie he most certainly died!

Adam experienced type of death number two, separation from God. You remember how God came walking in the garden in the cool of day as He had done before? When Adam and Eve heard Him coming they ran and hid themselves from him. At previous times they ran to Him. They'd had sweet fellowship with their Creator, but now something was different. When God came into the garden He called out: "Adam, where are you?" (As if God did not know)

Why did Adam go and hide himself from God when in times past he ran to God? What changed? Adam experienced death, separation from God. The fellowship that he had known before he ate of the fruit was broken. So yes Adam did die, just not immediately physically.

You remember that Adam told God that they were naked so they hid themselves. God said: "Who told you that you were naked? Have you eaten from the tree of which I commanded you not to eat?" The act of sin, in this case, disobedience brought separation from the fellowship and the presence of God.

Personally I believe that Adam and Eve were clothed with the glory of God before the fall, and that is why they never recognized their nakedness before.

Adam and Eve after realizing their nakedness sewed fig leaves together to cover their nakedness. Of course this would never do so God killed an animal and covered their nakedness with the skin of the dead animal, setting the standard that without the shedding of blood there is no forgiveness (Hebrews 9:22).

Personally I believe that Adam and Eve were clothed with the glory of God before the fall, and that is why they never recognized their nakedness before. Once the fellowship was broken and sin entered the human race the glory of God lifted off of them and they realized their condition.

Now go with me to the Garden of Gethsemane. Jesus was praying and pouring His heart out to the Father. You remember His anguish, as He did not want to go to the cross. He asked the Father to let this cup pass from Me. But never the less, not My will but Thy will be done!

Why was Jesus in such torment and agony over this decision? Was it just because of the agony, suffering and pain of the crucifixion on His body that He wanted to avoid or was there more?

We must keep in mind what happened on the cross, which Jesus knew was going to happen when He went:

"He made Him who knew no sin to be sin on our behalf, so that we might become the righteousness of God in Him."
2 Corinthians 5:21 NASB

Jesus knew that when He went to the cross that your sin and my sin would be placed upon Him. Even though He Himself never sinned, He would become sin. And just as sin caused a separation from God for the first Adam, so sin would cause a separation from God for the second Adam.

We must remember that in all of eternity past before His incarnation Jesus was always in perfect fellowship and harmony with the Father. He was there at the creation of this world when God said: "Let **Us** make man in **Our** image according to **Our** likeness." (Emphasis mine) We must also bear in mind that all through His earthly ministry, Jesus always did those things that were pleasing to the Father.

In fact on more than one occasion God uttered the words: "This is My beloved Son." **Matthew 3:17, 17:5** In fact Jesus himself said: "I must work the works of Him that sent me." And: "Truly, truly, I say to you, the Son can do nothing of Himself, unless it is something He sees the Father doing; for whatever the Father does, these things the Son also does in like manner." **John 5:19 NASB**

The culmination of this reality came on the cross when all of the sin of the whole world, past, present and future was placed on Jesus. He literally became sin. At that moment you remember Jesus cried: "My God, My God why have you forsaken Me?" **Mark 15:34** What Jesus knew was coming became a reality. He died spiritually first; He experienced separation from His Father.

As we follow the crucifixion account we find that Jesus knowing in Himself that all things had been fulfilled, He bowed His head and gave up His spirit. At this point He experienced physical death or the cessation of life. But we are not done yet…

Jesus Went To Hell

I know when I make that statement it ruffles a lot of religious feathers, but it is true just the same and thank God He did or we would still have to! Even the Apostles Creed tells us so:

"I believe in God, the Father Almighty, the Maker of heaven and earth, and in Jesus Christ, His only Son, our Lord: Who was conceived by the Holy Ghost, born of the virgin Mary, suffered under Pontius Pilate, was crucified, dead, and buried; **He descended into hell**. The third day He arose again from the dead; He ascended into heaven, and sitteth on the right hand of God the Father Almighty; from thence he shall come to judge the quick and the dead."

If Jesus were to truly redeem us from hell death and the grave…He must not just suffer spiritual death, separation from God; physical death, the cessation of life; but also judgment death or going to hell.

Let us examine a well-known verse of Scripture:

"*For the **wages** of **sin** is **death**, but the free gift of God is eternal life in Christ Jesus our Lord.*" **Romans 6:23 NASB**

What type of death is being referred to here in this text? As my Mother often says: "This is why when you read the Bible, you can't just read the Bible." If you don't know what type of death this Scripture is referring to you will have a skewed understanding.

Is it referring to physical death? Well, if it were the first time you lied to your parents as a child growing up, you would have fallen over dead. Is it referring to spiritual death? No, since the fall of Adam in the garden the Bible tells us that we are conceived in iniquity and born in sin, we are born physically already separated from God.

So obviously the type of death that is the wages of sin is judgment or damnation.

We have established that Jesus already experienced separation from God while on the cross and then the end of physical life, now He had to experience the third type of death, judgment or damnation. In order for Jesus to redeem us from all three types of death, he must have experienced all three types of death!

Consider with me Peter's message on the Day of Pentecost where he quotes from Psalm 16:10:

*"BECAUSE YOU WILL NOT **ABANDON MY SOUL TO HADES**, NOR ALLOW YOUR HOLY ONE TO UNDERGO DECAY"* **Acts 2:27 NASB**

*"He looked ahead and spoke of the resurrection of the Christ, that **HE WAS NEITHER ABANDONED TO HADES**, NOR DID His flesh SUFFER DECAY."* **Acts 2:31 NASB**

Did you notice what Peter said? He "will not abandon my soul to Hades." Abandoned has several meanings which include deserted, left or forsaken. In order to be abandoned or left somewhere that must mean that you are there. You can't be left in China if you are not in China. So therefore for Jesus to not be left in Hades, He must have been in Hades.

Then we can go to the writings of the Apostle Paul where he quotes from Psalm 68:18 for more clarification:

"Therefore it says, WHEN HE ASCENDED ON HIGH, **HE LED CAPTIVE A HOST OF CAPTIVES**, (He led a

parade of captives – New Century Version) *AND HE GAVE GIFTS TO MEN. Now this expression, 'He ascended,' what does it mean except that **He also had descended** into the lower parts of the earth?"* **Ephesians 2:8 & 9 NASB**

Notice Paul also talks about Jesus descending into the lower parts of the earth; other translations say depths of the earth or lowest parts of the earth. This is where the devil thought he won his ultimate victory, but it turned out to be his greatest defeat.

"But we speak God's wisdom in a mystery, the hidden wisdom which God predestined before the ages to our glory; the wisdom which none of the rulers of this age has understood; for if they had understood it they would not have crucified the Lord of glory." **I Corinthians 2:7 & 8 NASB**

This was a mystery that the enemy did not understand. All through Jesus' earthly life he tried to kill Him; once they were going to stone Him, but He walked through their midst; once they were going to push Him off a cliff, but He walked through their midst. And of course as a small child Joseph was warned to flee to Egypt to escape death. **John 8:59, Luke 4:29&30, Matthew 2:13** Now it seems the devil has won.

This is where the devil thought he won his ultimate victory, but it turned out to be his greatest defeat.

Don't you think the devil would have kept Jesus in hell if he could have? Why in the world would he let him out? The truth of the matter is there was nothing he could do to keep Jesus there. I am reminded of a song that Carmen used to sing called "Sunday's On The Way" where he sang about how the devil and his demons crucified the Lord but could not stop His resurrection even if they wanted to.

When Jesus was raised from the dead on Easter Sunday morning, it was not just a physical resurrection of His body coming out of the grave; but His spirit man was also raised up out of hell both by the power of the Holy Spirit.

*"But if the **Spirit of Him who raised Jesus from the dead** dwells in you, He who raised Christ Jesus from the dead will also give life to your mortal bodies through His Spirit who dwells in you."* **Romans 8:11 NASB**

Jesus the last Adam (1 Corinthians 15:45) was the first born again man by the power of the Holy Spirit. Remember, Jesus was separated, the fellowship with Father God broken on the cross, He was spiritually dead, and so he needed to be Born Again with the life and nature of God just like we do.

*"For those whom He foreknew, He also predestined to become conformed to the image of His Son, **so that He would be the firstborn among many brethren.**"* **Romans 8:29 NASB**

The Spirit of God raised Jesus from the dead, physically out of the grave, spiritually by giving him the life and nature of God again and from judgment as He raised Him out of hell. There were three resurrections on Easter Sunday not just one. (This is where I wish I were preaching this instead of writing it because right about now I would be coming unglued and losing all of my composure.)

The devil could not stop the resurrection and he could not keep Jesus in hell. After three days the Father said that's it, that's enough and the Holy Spirit re-energized Jesus with the life and nature of God. He became born again and came out of hell and He led a parade of all the Old Testament saints behind Him, as He was the drum major leading the procession. Remember what we read before... **HE LED CAPTIVE A HOST OF CAPTIVES**, (He led a parade of captives – New Century Version).

When Jesus came out, Moses was behind Him, Joshua was behind Him, David was behind Him, and Abraham was behind Him. And if that was not enough...on His way out He took the keys of hell, death and the grave!

"When I saw Him, I fell at His feet like a dead man. And He placed His right hand on me, saying, 'Do not be afraid; I am the first and the last, and the living One; and I was dead, ***and behold, I am alive forevermore, and I have the keys of death and of Hades.'"*** **Revelation 1:17 & 18 NASB**

This is the Prelude To Pentecost...What happened between IT IS FINISHED and HE IS RISEN. There was a battle in Hell that Satan lost and Christ won by the Power of The Holy Spirit that sealed our salvation and defeated hell, death and the grave. Now we can say with the Apostle Paul: *"O death, where is thy sting? O grave, where is thy victory?"* **I Corinthians 15:55 KJV**

Before we can examine what Satan saw on Pentecost we must have this foundation as a backdrop. The Holy Spirit blew the doors of hell wide open and ransacked his kingdom, and he was powerless to stop it. If we don't understand this...we miss Pentecost all together.

Chapter 2
The Pouring Of Pentecost

"Oh No Here It Comes Again!" This must have been what the devil was thinking when Acts Chapter 2 came to be. He just lived through the wind of the Spirit of God blowing through the region of the damned fifty days before, he is just about getting his bearings back and now that same wind is blowing again in the upper room.

Peter said in his sermon on the Day of Pentecost that this outpouring was the fulfillments of Joel's prophecy.

"And it shall come to pass in the last days, says God, That I **will pour out of My Spirit on all flesh**; *Your sons and your daughters shall prophesy, Your young men shall see visions, Your old men shall dream dreams"* **Acts 2:17 NKJV**

"And it shall come to pass afterward That **I will pour out My Spirit on all flesh**; *Your sons and your daughters shall prophesy, Your old men shall dream dreams, Your young men shall see visions. And also on My menservants and on My maidservants I will pour out My Spirit in those days."* **Joel 2:28 & 29 NKJV**

Joel prophesied of a time to come when the Holy Spirit would be poured out on all flesh. This was a new concept, for under the Old Covenant the Spirit only came upon the Prophet, the Priest or the King. This promise was for common folks, regardless of age, young or old, even on servants.

Even during Jesus ministry the devil really only had to worry about Jesus being endued with power from on high. Nobody else was carrying the anointing. Jesus received the power of the Holy Spirit at the baptism of John when the Father spoke and said: *"This is My beloved*

Son..." and the Spirit descended on Him in the form of a dove. (Matthew 3, Mark 1 and Luke 3)

Jesus was one man in one place at one time. He was limited to time and space, the laws of physical nature, since He came as a man.

*"...But **emptied Himself**, taking the form of a bond-servant, and being made in the likeness of men."* **Philippians 2:7 NASB**

The original Greek says...he laid aside equality with or the form of God. (New Testament Greek Lexicon) The footnote of the New American Standard Bible says...i.e. laid aside his privileges. The Message words it this way:

*"When the time came, **he set aside the privileges of deity** and took on the status of a slave, **became human!**"* **Philippians 2:7 The Message**

Weymouth put it this way: *"Nay, He **stripped Himself of His glory**, and took on Him the nature of a bondservant by **becoming a man like other men."*** **Philippians 2:7 WNT**

Jesus became just like all other humans, He emptied Himself, stripped Himself, set aside His deity and became like other men. Hebrews also bears out this truth...

*"Jesus understands every weakness of ours, **because he was tempted in every way that we are.** But he did not sin!"* **Hebrews 4:15 CEV**

If Jesus had not emptied Himself, but retained His Omnipotence, (Being all powerful) His Omniscience (Being all knowing) and His Omnipresence (Being present everywhere)...how could He be tempted in every way (or in all points NKJV) like us? It would be impossible to tempt Him if He had retained all of those things. Therefore Jesus was one man who could be in one place at one time who had the Holy Spirit poured out upon Him.

But now it is different. For the devil it went from a prophet, a priest or a king under the Old Covenant; to Jesus who was bridging the gap between the completion of the Old Covenant while establishing the New Covenant; to the beginning of the Church Age, where now the outpouring comes upon 120 believers all at the same time.

Thank God the outpouring of the Spirit is still for all flesh.

What we must understand is that just as Satan was powerless to stop the wind of the Spirit that blew through hell and resurrected Jesus out of there; he was powerless to stop the fulfillment of God's prophetic word through the Prophet Joel on the Day of Pentecost.

Now the Church Age has begun. Now the Scripture has been fulfilled. Now the beginning of the Last Days has been marked. (That is another whole teaching that we don't have time to go into here...but if Pentecost was the beginning of the Last Days, than we must certainly be in the last of the Last Days)

Thank God the outpouring of the Spirit is still for all flesh. All you have to do to qualify is have flesh. I thank God often that I have flesh and I qualify for the outpouring of the Spirit that started on the Day of Pentecost and continues through today.

So now the devil has lived through the Prelude to Pentecost, and he has seen the wind of the Spirit blow again in the Pouring of Pentecost, now comes...

Chapter 3
The Power Of Pentecost

"But you will receive power when the Holy Spirit has come upon you..." **Acts 1:8a NASB**

This of course is every preacher's favorite text to load up and let it rip on. (Preacher talk) If you can't get wound up and preach on this text, then you can't preach. This of course was Jesus' promise to the disciples just before His ascension.

There is only one Holy Spirit and only one Holy Spirit Power.

The Greek word for power in this text is the word "Dunamis", which means:
* Strength, power, ability.
* Inherent power, power residing in a thing by virtue of its nature.
* Power for performing miracles.
* Explosive power.
* Self-energizing power.

The Amplified Bible renders it this way:

"But you shall receive power (ability, efficiency, and might) when the Holy Spirit has come upon you..." **Acts 1:8a AMP**

Remember that Jesus commanded His followers to tarry in Jerusalem until they be endued with power from on high (Luke 24:49). The Day of Pentecost fulfilled this promise. When the Holy Spirit was poured out the "Dunamis" power of the Spirit was released.

Which Holy Spirit was released? Which power of the Holy Spirit was released? You are probably thinking: "Mike you have lost your mind, there is only one Holy Spirit and only one Holy Spirit power." That is exactly right! The Holy Spirit that was poured out on Pentecost was the same Holy Spirit that came upon Jesus as a dove at the Baptism of John.

The same Holy Spirit that raised Jesus from the dead was the same Holy Spirit that was poured out on Pentecost. The same power that raised Jesus from the dead was the same power that was poured out on Pentecost. It was immediately evident that the power was released.

Evidence Of The Power Number One

The first evidence we see is Peter's first recorded sermon in Acts chapter 2. Peter the disciple, who denied that he even know Christ, in fact swore that he did not know him, becomes Apostle Peter the bold preacher! Look at how boldly Peter gets everyone's attention:

"But Peter, taking his stand with the eleven, raised his voice and declared to them: "Men of Judea and all you who live in Jerusalem, let this be known to you and give heed to my words." **Acts 2:14 NASB**

Could this be the same Peter that denied he even knew Christ to the servant girl? (Matthew 26:69 & 70) Yes it is one and the same Peter! What made the difference in his life? I submit that it is the Power of Pentecost that was released.

Evidence Of The Power Number Two

The second evidence may be a bit different than you have thought:

"And they were all filled with the Holy Spirit and began to speak with other tongues, as the Spirit was giving them utterance." **Acts 2:4 NASB**

I know what you are thinking: "Mike how in the world can those speaking in tongues be an evidence of Holy Spirit power?" I am so glad you asked! Have you ever read?

"One who speaks in a tongue edifies himself..." **1 Corinthians 14:4a NASB**

The New Living Translation says: "Is strengthened personally". Holman Christian Standard Bible says: "Builds himself up." The word translated edifies in most translations in the original Greek means to build or charge up.

It is a word that we really don't use too much in our everyday speech these days. The picture is of a car battery that gets run down and won't start the car. You can then take the battery and put in on a battery charger and "edify" it (or build it back up again).

That is exactly what happens when a believer prays in their prayer language (or other tongues or in the Holy Spirit, you can use whichever term you like). As you pray in tongues you build yourself up or make yourself stronger.

Before the Day of Pentecost this was a manifestation of the Holy Spirit, which had not yet been seen or experienced. Most New Testament believers believe that Tongues and the Interpretation of Tongues were saved specifically for the Church Age or dispensation. (This book is not the place to go into a discourse on these gifts, perhaps a later book will deal with these things in great detail.)

On this particular day Peter was a changed man.

Evidence Of The Power Number Three

The third evidence we see of the power comes in the very next chapter of the book of Acts, in chapter three. Here we have the encounter of the lame beggar at the Gate Beautiful with Peter and John as they are going up at the hour of prayer.

We all know this story well. This man was lame from his mother's womb and every day he was set at the temple gate to beg alms for the poor. On this particular day Peter was a changed man. I am sure that he had passed this beggar before since he was laid there daily and this was not the first time Peter was coming to the temple at the hour of prayer.

On this day however, something was different, Peter had just been endued with power from on high, and he had just received power after the Holy Spirit came upon him. Now Peter reacts to the beggar in a way he never had before. Previously I am sure he just walked by. Maybe he might have dropped a coin or two. But now it is different...

Peter again with new holy boldness, (which he just received) says to the beggar: "Look at us". I am sure at this point Peter had the beggar's undivided attention. He was sure he was about to get some money, or so he thought. Imagine how the wind must have been let out of his sails when Peter says: "Silver and Gold have I none."

I can just imagine the beggar thinking to himself: "Boy you are some piece of work, you tell me to look at you,

you get my hopes up and now you tell me that you don't have anything to give me. Why in the world are you telling me to look at you?"

At this point Peter says: "But what I have I give thee, in the Name of Jesus Christ of Nazareth rise up and walk." Now Peter takes him by the hand and in my head I visualize Peter jerking him up from the ground, as the "Dunamis" power of God hits the beggar and instantly his anklebones receive strength and he goes into the temple leaping and dancing and praising God.

What made the difference in Peter? The Power of Pentecost. What will make the difference in us? The Power of Pentecost.

So now the devil has lived through the Prelude to Pentecost, and he has seen the wind of the Spirit blow again in the Pouring of Pentecost, and he has seen the effects of the Power of Pentecost, now comes...

Chapter 4
The Problem Of Pentecost

Remember we are writing this book from Satan's perspective. We are looking at Pentecost, as he must have viewed it. From our point of view, Pentecost is no problem at all. But from the devil's point of view Pentecost is one big Problem.

Folks I have to tell you at this point Mr. Devil is having a BAD DAY! You want to talk about needing Extra Strength Excedrin…I don't think that would have helped him one bit. His Problem is bad and fixing to get worse.

When Jesus was on the earth, He was the only one the devil had to deal with who had Holy Ghost Power. But now that the Holy Spirit was poured out in the upper room on the 120, he had 120 little Jesus' filled with that same power that fifty days before tore his kingdom apart when Jesus was raised up.

Folks I have to tell you at this point Mr. Devil is having a
BAD DAY!

The devil could not stop this. God had already declared that it was coming by the Prophet Joel and now it has been fulfilled, everyday common Christians just like you and I are being and can be filled with the Power of the Holy Spirit. No longer for just the Prophet, Priest or King; but anyone, just someone with flesh could receive this power.

As we go through the book of Acts we find how the devil's problem gets compounded with each passing day.

*"So then, those who had received his word were baptized; and **that day there were added about three thousand souls.**"* **Acts 2:41 NASB**

The first compounding of the problem for the devil is that it goes from 120 to 3120 in one day as 3000 souls are added after Peter's sermon.

*"Day by day continuing with one mind in the temple, and breaking bread from house to house, they were taking their meals together with gladness and sincerity of heart, praising God and having favor with all the people. **And the Lord was adding to their number day by day those who were being saved.**"* **Acts 2: 46 & 47 NASB**

Now it goes from 120 to 3120 to the Lord adding daily those who are being saved.

Notice that this is some of the same bunch that got filled in the upper room.

---

*"And when they had prayed, the place where they had gathered together was shaken, **and they were all filled with the Holy Spirit** and began to speak the word of God with boldness."* **Acts 4:31 NASB**

Notice that this is some of the same bunch that got filled in the upper room. Why are they now being filled again if they were filled in Acts chapter 2? Because we leak. Paul told us in Ephesians 5:19 to be filled with the Holy Spirit. However in the original Greek, what it really says is: "Always be being filled with the Holy Spirit".

It was written in what is known as a continuous tense. We should always be being filled. And because we see that that they were filled in Acts Chapter 2 and then again in Acts chapter 4, we know that God has made it possible for us to do just that. He would never tell us to do something that we could not do or that He had not made provision for.

*"And in those days, when the **number of the disciples was multiplied**...And the word of God increased; and the **number of the disciples multiplied** in Jerusalem greatly..."* **Acts 6:1a & 7a KJV**

Now we see that it goes from souls being added to the church to the number of disciples being multiplied. I can imagine the devil thinking: "Man they're like guppies, they're like rabbits, and they're multiplying". Folks, he is having a bad day.

*"But the word of the Lord continued to grow and to **be multiplied**."* **Acts 12:24 NASB**

Again we see that it has gone beyond addition and is continuing in multiplication.

The devil's problem went from dealing with one man, Jesus, filled with the power of the Holy Spirit, who could only be in one place at one time, to having to deal with multiplied thousands who had access to this same power that destroyed his kingdom and could be all over the earth simultaneously.

For example, in 1993 shortly after I returned from Oklahoma to New Jersey to work with my Parents in ministry, I took a short-term missionary trip to Africa. I spent about two and a half weeks in Uganda and about two and a half weeks in Kenya. At the same time my Mom and Dad were living in Trinidad running a Bible College and overseeing a minister's fellowship on the island.

Now at exactly the same time, I was in Africa doing crusades, conferences and seminars anointed by the

Holy Spirit seeing people get saved, healed, delivered, filled with the Holy Spirit and set free; my Folks were in Trinidad training up and coming ministers in the Bible College and ministering out in churches and crusades anointed by the Holy Spirit seeing people get saved, healed, delivered, filled with the Holy Spirit and set free.

This is just one example on a very small scale. Imagine that worldwide by how many Born Again, Spirit Filled Believers there are alive on this planet right now that all have the potential because of the Pouring and the Power of Pentecost to really give the devil a really big Problem.

Final Thoughts

Well if you were the devil what would you do? Because of the problem that he is now facing, he goes back to his bag of tricks and does what he has always done. The Bible says that he is a liar and the father of lies (John 8:44). So he begins to spin some false doctrines to keep the people of God from walking in what He has provided for them.

Spin is not an unusual concept in our day and age. All you have to do is turn on a newscast and you are guaranteed to see and hear some spin. You have what the politician said…and then comes the spin from the pundits, prognosticators and commentators as to what the politician meant when they said what they said.

Depending on where you get your news will determine which type of spin you get. Certain networks and media outlets spin to the right. Most networks and media outlets spin to the left. But based on what we see everyday…we should all understand that spin is not the truth!

Just for the record…I am not saying that all news people and pundits are the devil, just that sometimes they act like him by spinning the truth.

Lie Number One

"This experience is not for today, it died with the apostles."

I don't know how many of you have heard this one before…but the early days of my Christian life I believed it, defended it, perpetuated it and taught it. I was raised as a Baptist boy and like most Baptist's we were cessationists.

All that simply means is that you believe all the supernatural power of God that you see in the Bible does not happen anymore. Everything that occurred in the book of Acts ceased to be with the passing of the New Testament Apostles. God can do the supernatural if He wants to, after all He is sovereign, but we really don't expect Him to and thus He doesn't and He won't.

We used to pray prayers like: "Lord if it be Your will, heal Aunt Suzie." The unfortunate end to that prayer... although never verbalized was: "If it isn't let her die." And most of the time she did.

Now you may be one who has never been sold this bill of goods and for your sake I hope you haven't. But, many dear saints of God who love Him with all their hearts, souls, mind and strength have. They have had well meaning teachers and preachers who have had to explain away a powerless Christian life resort to pulling Scripture out of context to fit their dilemma.

The way that one arrives at this position is from a well-known portion of Scripture.

"Love never fails; but if there are <u>gifts of prophecy</u>, they will be <u>done away</u>; if there are <u>tongues</u>, they <u>will cease</u>; if there is <u>knowledge</u>, it will be <u>done away</u>. For we know in part and we prophesy in part; but **when the perfect comes, the partial will be done away."** **I Corinthians 13:8-10 NASB** (Emphasis mine)

You may be asking how that type of a doctrine can be supported from this text of Scripture. HERE IS THE SPIN:

1. If there is Prophecy...it will be done away.
2. If there are tongues...they will cease.
3. If there is knowledge...it will be done away.
4. When the perfect comes...the partial will be done away.

5. The perfect that is to come was fulfilled with the completion of the Canon of Scripture.
6. Now that we have the Complete Canon...we no longer need: prophecy, tongues or knowledge.

Now you may look at that and say to yourself, there is no way to get that interpretation out of that Scripture text. I agree with you now, but there was a time in my life that I not only believed it, but I was taught it, and I defended it.

We must remember that faith comes by hearing whether good or bad. If we hear correct doctrine, we will have faith in correct doctrine. But, if we are taught false doctrine, we will have faith in false doctrine. Someone once said you are what you eat; that is just as true spiritually as it is physically.

It is obvious that Paul in this text is showing the limitations of prophetic gifting. No one of us knows it all and no one of us understands it all. That is why: "We know in part and we prophesy in part." Thank God for the part that He reveals to you. Thank God for the part that He reveals to your brother or your sister. If I get one part and you get one part, and he gets one part, and she gets one part, and we all put all of our parts together we get a much fuller picture of what God is revealing.

The perfect that is to come is certainly not the completion of the canon of Scripture. This is a case where one must apply the solid principles of Hermeneutics; which simply is the art and science of Bible interpretation. Paul said to rightly divide the 'Word Of Truth', which must mean that one can wrongly divide the 'Word Of Truth'.

"I thank my God always concerning you for the grace of God which was given you in Christ Jesus, that in everything you

were enriched in Him, in all speech and all knowledge, even as the testimony concerning Christ was confirmed in you, so that you are not lacking in any gift, awaiting eagerly the revelation of our Lord Jesus Christ." **I Corinthians 1:4-7 NASB** (Emphasis mine)

Notice that Paul is writing to the same church here in this text. This is chapter I of his first letter to the Corinthians. Did you see that they were not lacking in any of the gifts, and that they were eagerly waiting the REVELATION OF THE LORD JESUS CHRIST? The King James says: "...waiting for the coming of our Lord Jesus Christ." The New Living Translation renders verse 7 this way:

"*Now you have every spiritual gift you need as you eagerly wait for the return of our Lord Jesus Christ.*" **I Corinthians 1:7 NLT** (Emphasis mine)

Here Paul is connecting spiritual gifts with the return of the Lord Jesus Christ. If we go further into chapter 13 of I Corinthians we will see a fuller explanation.

"*When I was a child, I used to speak like a child, think like a child, reason like a child; when I became a man, I did away with childish things. For now we see in a mirror dimly,* **but then face to face**; *now I know in part,* **but then I will know fully just as I also have been fully known.**" **I Corinthians 13:11 & 12 NASB** (Emphasis mine)

When will I see Him face to face? When I know just as I am fully known? At the return of the Lord Jesus! What Paul is stressing is that these gifts are limited but necessary, and we need them until the Perfect One, The Lord Jesus Christ comes, then we won't need them anymore.

Lie Number Two

"Speaking in tongues is of the devil."

Again, I am not sure how many of you have heard this one before...but not only have I heard it, at one time in my life I believed it as well. Let's face it...if we think that something is of the devil, no self-respecting Christian would ever want to do it. So if the devil has Christians convinced that speaking in tongues is of him they would never want to speak in tongues.

I know, I know, I can hear what you are thinking: "Now Mike why is speaking in tongues so important?" I am so glad you asked that question...

"For one who speaks in a tongue does not <u>speak to men but to God</u>; for no one understands, but in <u>his spirit he speaks mysteries</u>." **I Corinthians 14:2 NASB** (Emphasis mine)

Weymouth in his translation renders the last line: *"... **Yet in the Spirit he is speaking secret truths.**"* **I Corinthians 14:2b WNT** (Emphasis mine)

When you speak or pray in tongues you are speaking to God not men. It is important that we point out here that there is a difference between: Your prayer language and The Public Gift of Tongues (I Corinthians 12:10), which must be interpreted. (In this context we are talking about your prayer language, not the public gift.)

When you speak in the public gift of tongues you are speaking to men.

No one understands your prayer language, not even you. In the Spirit you are speaking mysteries, secret truths; one old translation said divine secrets.

"One who speaks in a tongue edifies himself..."
I Corinthians 14:4a NASB

When you speak or pray in tongues you edify yourself, we have already discussed this earlier so we will move on.

"Now I wish that you all spoke in tongues..."
I Corinthians 14:5a NASB

If speaking in tongues were of the devil, why would Paul wish that everyone did it? Certainly he would not want everyone to do something that was of the devil.

"For if I pray in a tongue, my spirit prays, but my mind is unfruitful." **I Corinthians 14:14 NASB**

When I pray in tongues, it is my spirit that is praying not my mind. Remember we are three part beings: Spirit (heart or inner-man), Soul (mind, will and emotions) and Body (Earthly Tabernacle).

Our mind is unfruitful or does not understand when we pray in tongues because it is not involved only our spirit is.

"I thank God; I speak in tongues more than you all."
I Corinthians 14:18 NASB

Why would Paul thank God that he did something more than all the rest of the Corinthian church put together if it was of the devil?

"Therefore, my brethren, desire earnestly to prophesy, and do not forbid to speak in tongues." **I Corinthians 14:39 NASB**

Certainly if speaking in tongues were of the devil than Paul would have said to forbid speaking in tongues...but since he said forbid not to speak in tongues, obviously it can not be from the devil.

Thank God the Word of God is true and the lies and spin of the devil are just that...lies and spin. All that happened on the Day of Pentecost is still for today. All of the things that added up to a major problem for the devil on Pentecost are still a problem for him today.

In fact not only can we be initially filled (Baptized) with the Spirit, but there can be multiple and subsequent fillings. This enables us to always be being filled with the Holy Spirit. (Ephesians 5:18 Greek meaning)

The reason that the enemy has fought so hard against Pentecost and the Pentecostal experience is because:

PENTECOST ENFORCES THE VICTORY OF THE HOLY SPIRIT IN THE RESURRECTION OF THE LORD JESUS CHRIST!

EVERY TIME YOU PRAY IN TONGUES YOU REMIND THE DEVIL OF THE POWER OF THE HOLY SPIRIT!

ONE MORE TIME HE HAS TO RELIVE THE PRELUDE TO PENTECOST, THE POURING OF PENTECOST, THE POWER OF PENTECOST AND THE PROBLEM OF PENTECOST!

Notes

Notes

About The Author

Michael has been serving the Lord in active ministry for 30 years. He grew up in a Christian home, the son of two Ministers of the Gospel, and came to know the Lord as a child.

He was mentored and trained for the ministry in their home as a teenager before getting married at 20 and moving to Tulsa, OK to further his ministry training under Rev. Kenneth Hagin at Rhema Bible Training Center.

After graduation from Rhema in 1987, Michael began taking short-term missions trips to the nations. To date he has ministered in six different nations, some multiple times. Michael also furthered his ministerial training serving in many aspects of helps ministry at Victory Christian Center, Tulsa, OK, under Pastor Billy Joe Daugherty.

Since moving back to NJ in 1992, Michael has been a Staff Minister of Living Faith Ministries International, where he has served as an Evangelist, Revivalist, Missionary, Bible School Teacher and Trainer. For ten years he was actively involved at Oasis Christian Center (formerly Evangelistic Centre) in Rahway, NJ, as an Elder and Director of Adult Education under Pastor Fred McCarthy

In 2000 Michael's ministry began to change as God started to transition him from the Office of Evangelist to the Office of Prophet. Today he is a proven Minister as a House Prophet and part of the Apostolic Ministry Team at Community Church Fixer Of Hearts. He ministers the Word by both teaching and preaching in a powerful practical way. He specializes in teaching and training on the Gifts of The Holy Spirit and Prophetic Ministry.

Michael is currently serving in an Apostolic & Prophetic Ministry, under the covering of Apostles Leo & Edith Fram, and ministering in churches, seminars, crusades and short-term missions trips at the Lord's direction. He is in relationship with Apostle Frank Dupree from Metro Apostolic Network and John & Sheryl Price from NJ Global Apostolic Prayer Network. His desire is to see all members of the Body of Christ fulfill their individual destiny.

Contact Information

You may write Michael at:
Living Faith Ministries Int'l
PO Box 327
Brick, NJ 08723
USA

Via Email:
michael@livingfaithministriesintl.org

Via Our Ministry Website:
www.livingfaithministriesintl.org

CPSIA information can be obtained at www.ICGtesting.com
Printed in the USA
BVOW080416310513

322064BV00001B/42/P